Project Editor Sue Grabham
Senior Contributing Editor Charlotte Evans
Assistant Editor Tara Benson
Section Editors Jill Thomas, Angela Holroyd

Senior Designer Janice English
Staff Designer Siân Williams
Additional Design Smiljka Surla

Publishing Director Jim Miles

Art Director Paul Wilkinson

Additional Art Preparation
Matthew Gore, Andy Archer, Shaun Deal,
Julian Ewart, Narinder Sahotay, Andy Stanford,
Janet Woronkowicz

Picture Research Elaine Willis
Artwork Archivist Wendy Allison
Artwork Researcher Robert Perry

Activity Artist Caroline Jayne Church

Indexer Hilary Bird

Photo credits
7 Mansell Collection;
10 Ronald Grant Archive/DC Comics;
14 Mary Evans Picture Library;
19 Ronald Grant Archive;
49 Mary Evans Picture Library

Production Manager Linda Edmonds
Production Assistant Stephen Lang

Contributing Authors
Florence and Pierre-Olivier Wessels

Specialist Consultants
Dr Elizabeth McCall Smith MB, ChB, MRCGP,
DRCOG (General Practitioner, Edinburgh);
Julia Stanton BA DipEd (Australasia consultant)

Educational Consultants
Ellie Bowden (Curriculum Advisor for
Primary Science and Senior Teacher, Essex);
June Curtis (Primary School Teacher, Nottingham
and R.E. writer);
Kirsty Jack (Head Teacher, Primary
School, Edinburgh)

KINGFISHER
An imprint of Larousse plc
Elsley House, 24-30 Great Titchfield Street, London W1P 7AD

First published by Larousse plc 1994
Reprinted 1997

A CIP catalogue record for this book is available from the British Library

ISBN 0 7534 0152 5

Typeset by Tradespools Ltd, Frome, Somerset
Colour separation by P&W Graphics, Singapore
Printed in Hong Kong by
South China Printing Company (1988) Limited

KINGFISHER

Child's World

My Body

Kingfisher

Activities

Before you start each activity, collect everything you need and make sure there is a clear space. Remember to wear gloves when touching soil, and an apron for gluing, cooking and using paints. Use round-ended scissors for cutting, and if an adult is needed, ask if they can help before you start.

Afterwards, make sure you clear up any mess and put everything away.

▷Here are some of the materials that you might need for the activities. **Always** ask an adult before using anything that is not yours.

You will find lots of exciting things in this book to do and make.

Before you start cooking
- put on an apron
- wash your hands
- ask an adult to be nearby if you are cooking with a saucepan, or to put the oven on for you if you are baking food.

My Body

One person, one body

Adults and babies, boys and girls are all human beings. Their bodies are made the same way, but they are all different. No two human beings look exactly the same. People who belong to the same family are more alike than other people. Twins are most alike.

◁ In a family, people often look alike. Children and their parents may have hair and eyes that are the same colour.

▽ This is a family tree. It shows three generations of the same family. A generation is people of about the same age.

Word box
Human beings are the vast, world-wide family of men, women and children.
Generations are humans of about the same age. Grandparents are one generation, parents the next and children the next.

grandfather | grandmother

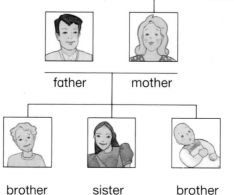

father   mother   uncle   aunt

brother   sister   brother   cousin

"Here I am!"

◁ There are human beings almost everywhere on Earth. They are of many sizes, shapes and colours. Human bodies all work in the same way, but they are all different. No one else is exactly the same as you.

Tweedledum and Tweedledee

Tweedledum and Tweedledee are characters in Lewis Carroll's story, Alice Through the Looking Glass. *They were identical twins who looked so alike that Alice could not tell them apart.*

△ The colour of our hair and skin, the shape of our eyes, ears, nose and chin all make us look different from one another. The shapes of our faces make us different too.

A body for living

The body is like a clever machine that can do lots of things. It can laugh, cry, talk, run, think, work and play. The body has adapted, or changed, to live in different places. But there are times when our bodies cannot adapt. We need special equipment under the sea, in the sky and in Space.

▽ There are so many things that the human body can do. What are the people doing in this park?

△ Clothes help the body to stay warm in cold places. The more clothes you wear, the warmer you are.

△ In hot countries, you do not need warm clothes. But you do need to cover your body, to protect it from the sun.

Can you find?

1 hang glider   5 submarine
2 swimmer   6 mountain
3 scuba diver
4 Space shuttle

▷ When we play some sports, we wear special clothes such as a helmet and pads to protect our bodies.

9

Body parts

The human body is made up of different parts. At the top is a head, with hair on it. The head is on a neck. Below that is a torso. This is the middle part of the body. We have two arms and two legs that are joined to the torso. Arms and legs are also called limbs. These parts of the body help it to do different things.

Your body

Your body is a wonderful machine with many parts. Each part has a special job and all the parts work together to keep you healthy. Like all machines your body needs fuel – food and drink. The oxygen you breathe in from the air helps turn the food you eat into energy. This energy allows you to play, work, think and grow. Exercise is important. It helps you to feel fit, look good and stay healthy. It also strengthens your muscles and helps to keep the blood flowing throughout your whole body.

Superman

Superman is a story character. He is very strong and can fly faster than any aircraft. He has X-ray vision, which means he can see through anything. He uses his special powers to help others in the world.

Word box

Torso is the main part of the human body, to which the head, arms and legs are attached.
Limbs are the arms and legs of human beings and other animals.

△ Hair protects our head. It helps keep it warm in winter and stops it from burning in the summer sun.

▽ We have feet at the bottom of our legs. Our feet are flat so that we can stand on them and walk upright.

What are you made of?

Most of your body is water. The rest is a mixture of chemicals. The water and chemical mix is arranged in tiny things called cells. Cells make up your skin, muscles, nerves, bones, blood and all the other parts of your body. Cells are so small they can only be seen by using a microscope. Although all the cells have things in common they do not all look the same. There are several hundred different kinds of cells in the body. The smallest cells are red blood cells. They carry food to all the other cells in the body.

▷ Our head is on our neck. The neck bends and turns. This means that our head can move up and down and from side to side.

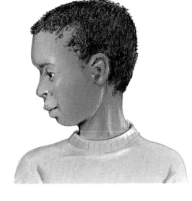

◁ Our neck, arms and legs are attached to our torso. This is the largest part of the body. It can twist, turn and bend in the middle.

▷ We move on our legs. They are long and strong. Legs let us stand upright and walk, run and jump.

▽ Our arms can bend and stretch. We use them to reach for things and use our hands to hold them.

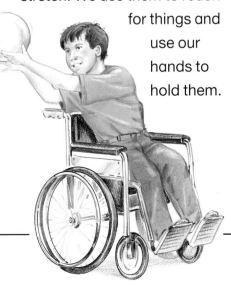

"Simon Says" game

One person is Simon. Simon faces the other players and says, "Simon says pat your head" (or similar). The rest copy. If Simon says, "Pat your toes" without "Simon says" first, the rest stand still. Anyone who moves is out. The last person left is Simon next time.

The skin

Skin covers the whole body. It keeps the parts inside us safe. Skin is tough, but it can also be hurt. It can be burned, cut or bruised. If skin is broken, it will bleed. Skin is not always the same colour. A brown colouring, called melanin, helps protect the skin from sunlight. Black skin has more melanin than white skin.

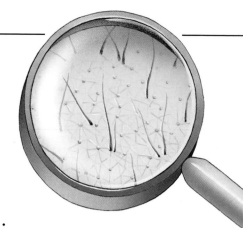

△ When you look at skin under a magnifying glass, it is not smooth. It has bumps on it and small holes. Hairs grow through these holes.

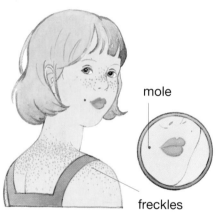

mole

freckles

△ Freckles and moles are patches of extra melanin on the skin. Freckles can come and go, but moles stay.

△ Skin may be burned by the sun. It goes red, then peels off. Skin can be protected with sunscreen creams.

▷ Sometimes our skin changes colour. We may go white if we are frightened and red if we are embarrassed.

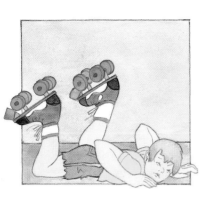

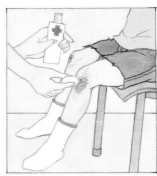

▽ A bandage keeps the wound clean. The blood dries up and new skin grows.

△ If you fall down, you sometimes break your skin, or graze it. Grazed skin bleeds.

△ The graze can be cleaned with a disinfectant to get rid of dirt and germs.

▽ Marks appear on our skin when it is hurt in any way. These marks have different names, depending on what caused them. They look different too.

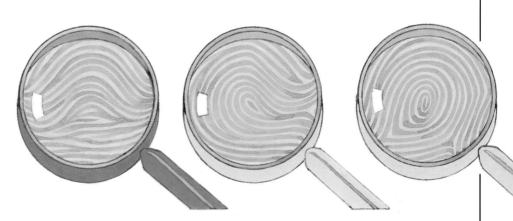

△ Every person in the world has their own special fingerprint pattern.

callus   blister

pinch mark

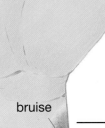

bruise

Make fingerprints

Lightly rub a thin coating of lipstick onto your fingertip. Press the fingertip on a piece of paper. It will leave a print. Do the same for your friends. Now look at the prints through a magnifying glass and see how different they are.

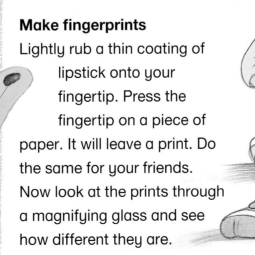

Hair and nails

We have hair all over our bodies, except for our palms and the soles of our feet. A lot of this hair is too fine to see easily. Hair grows thickest on our heads.

Nails protect our toes and fingertips. Our hair and nails are both made from a substance called keratin.

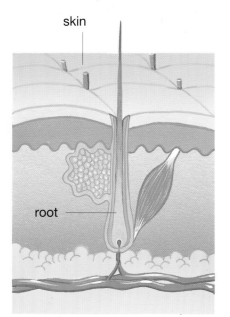
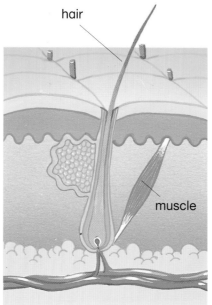

Rapunzel
(A story by the Brothers Grimm)

A witch shut Rapunzel in a tower. A prince climbed up her long hair to rescue her.

◁ You see only part of the hair. The rest is under the skin and is called the root. When you are cold, a little muscle pulls the hair upright.

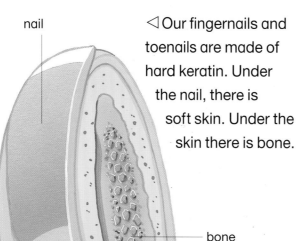

◁ Our fingernails and toenails are made of hard keratin. Under the nail, there is soft skin. Under the skin there is bone.

straight   wavy   curly

△ Some hair grows straight, some grows wavy and some grows curly. It comes in lots of different colours too.

Muscles

Our muscles are under our skin. We use muscles whenever we move. Muscles are joined to our bones. They move by becoming shorter or longer. Muscles move every part of the body, not just the bones. Our face muscles move our mouths. Our chest muscles help us to breathe.

△ The muscles in our face help us smile, frown, wink and chew. When we smile, we may use fifteen different muscles.

△ Muscles grow bigger and stronger with exercise and training. Athletes and people who play sports often have strong muscles.

▷ We have more than 650 muscles. There are muscles in every part of our body.

Find the answers

How many muscles do we use when we smile?

What makes muscles grow strong?

Bones and joints

There are over 200 bones in your body. Together, they form the skeleton. Bones support the body and give it shape. They also protect the soft organs inside the body. The places where the bones meet are called joints. Bones are very strong, but they can break.

Find the answers

What is the tip of your nose made of?

Name four joints.

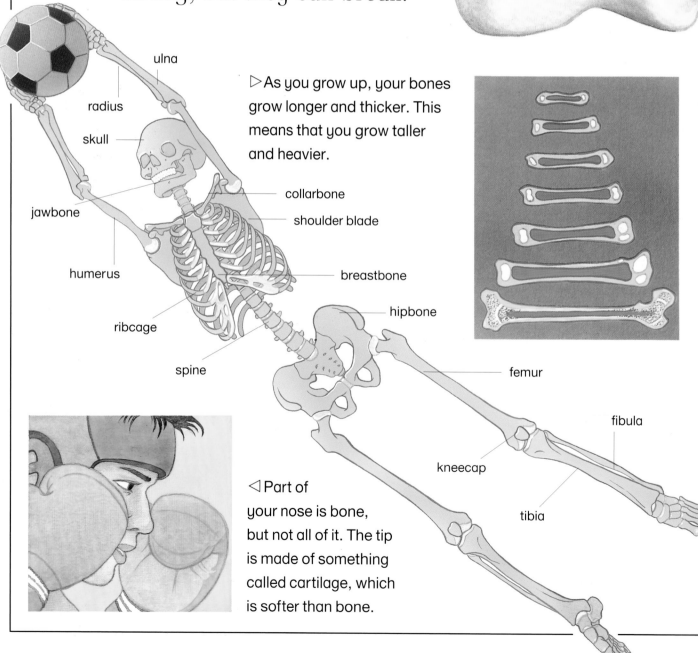

ulna

radius

skull

jawbone

humerus

ribcage

spine

▷ As you grow up, your bones grow longer and thicker. This means that you grow taller and heavier.

collarbone

shoulder blade

breastbone

hipbone

femur

fibula

kneecap

tibia

◁ Part of your nose is bone, but not all of it. The tip is made of something called cartilage, which is softer than bone.

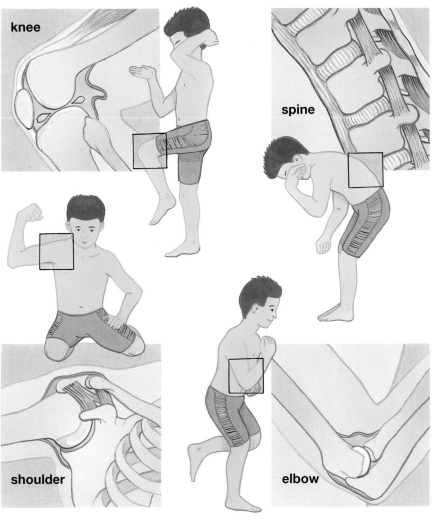

knee

spine

shoulder

elbow

△ Our knees, spine, shoulders and elbows are some of the joints where bones meet. Some bones fit together, others slide over each other.

Make a scary skeleton costume

Draw bone shapes, like the ones below, on a large sheet of white paper. Cut them out. Safety pin the bones to a black T-shirt and black leggings. Then put the clothes on. When you lift your arms and legs the skeleton will move.

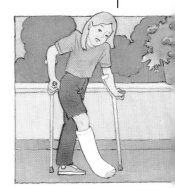

△ Bones may break in a fall. A broken bone is called a fracture.

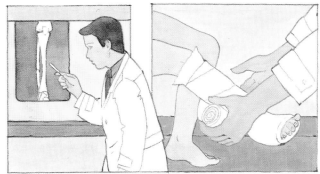

△ A doctor X-rays the bone to see the break.

△ Plaster holds the bone straight while it grows back together again.

Body organs

There are soft parts called organs inside your body. They are protected by the bones and skin. The organs include the brain, lungs, liver, heart, pancreas, kidneys, stomach and intestines. Each of the organs has a special job to do. The brain tells all the other organs what to do. Together, they help the body to work properly.

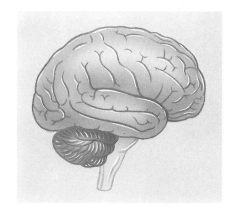

△ The brain is very important because it tells your body how to work. It controls all the other organs.

▷ The brain is in the head. Other organs are in the torso, the main part of the body. They are all different shapes, but they fit together very neatly.

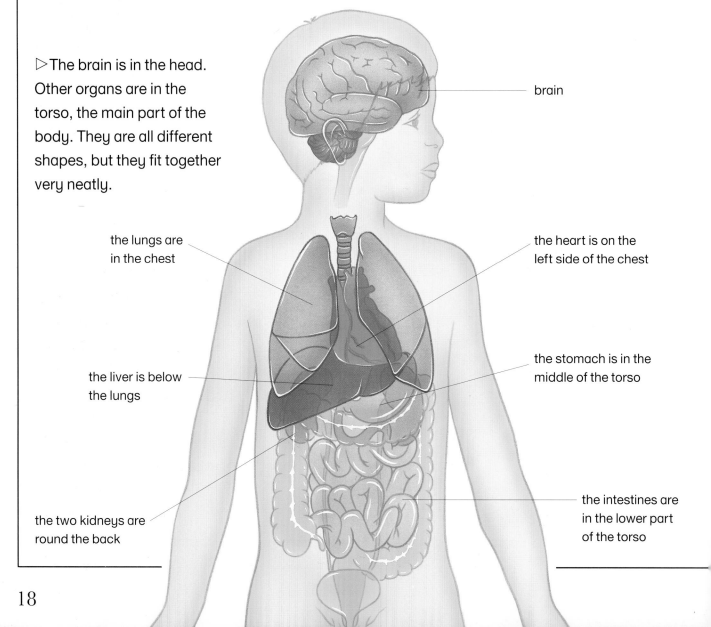

brain

the lungs are in the chest

the heart is on the left side of the chest

the liver is below the lungs

the stomach is in the middle of the torso

the two kidneys are round the back

the intestines are in the lower part of the torso

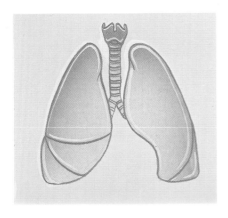

△ We breathe with our lungs. They take air into the body.

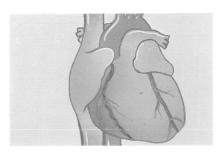

△ The heart pumps blood around the body.

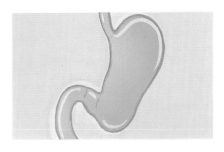

△ The food we eat goes down into the stomach. It turns the food into a pulp before it goes into the intestines.

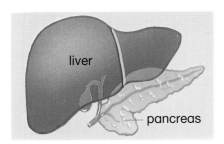

△ The liver and pancreas help us to digest our food.

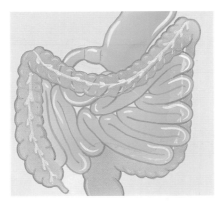

△ The intestines pass liquid food into the blood.

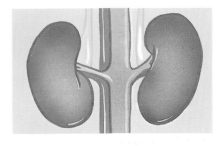

△ Two kidneys help to get rid of the waste from our blood and produce urine from it.

The Wizard of Oz
(A story by L. Frank Baum)

In The Wizard of Oz, *Dorothy meets some characters who have organs missing. Tin Man has no heart and Straw Man has no brain. In this picture from the film, you can see Dorothy and Straw Man on the yellow brick road. They all travel along the yellow brick road in search of the Wizard, who they hope will help them.*

How are we made?

The body is made of lots of tiny living parts called cells. Before we are born we all begin as one cell inside our mother's body. A baby grows in a place called the womb. Genes are parts of the cell that tell it how to grow. Every baby has genes from both the mother's and father's cells.

△ Every baby is made by a man and a woman. They are called its parents.

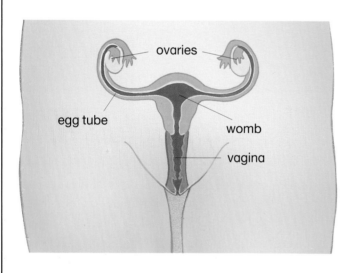

△ These are the organs which a woman has to make a baby. The ovaries produce eggs.

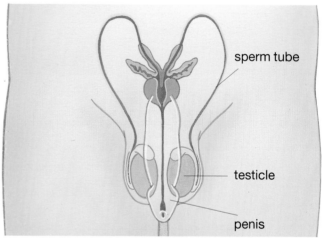

△ These are the organs which a man has to make a baby. The testicles produce sperm.

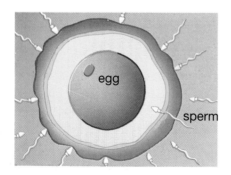

△ A sperm enters an egg. This makes the baby's first cell.

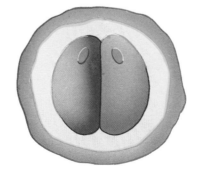

△ The egg splits into two cells. It will then split into four.

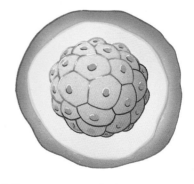

△ It goes on splitting and grows bigger and bigger.

▷A doctor or a special nurse called a midwife checks that the baby is growing properly in its mother's womb. A scanning machine shows the baby inside her.

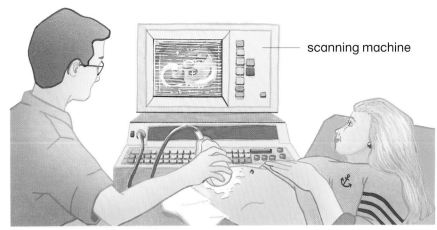

scanning machine

◁Sometimes a mother has two babies from one egg. They are identical twins. Identical twins are two boys or two girls who look just like each other.

▷A mother may also have twins from two eggs. These twins are not identical. The children do not grow up to look alike.

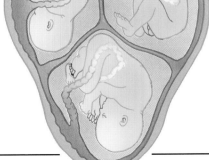

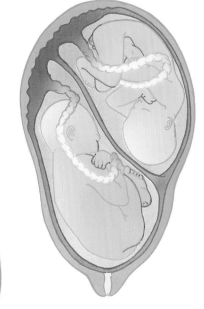

◁Sometimes a mother may have three, four, five or six babies. This is very rare. It is called a multiple birth.

Word box
Cells are tiny living parts that make up our bodies.
Genes are the instructions in cells that decide how living things will develop.
Womb is the place inside the mother where a baby grows until it is born.

Nine months for a baby

The baby grows in a bag of warm liquid in the mother's womb. It gets all the food and oxygen it needs from its mother's body, through a tube called the umbilical cord. After nine months, the baby is born. The mother may give birth in a hospital.

▽ When a baby is about three months old it looks like this. This is a life-size picture.

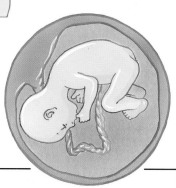

 a sperm enters an egg to make the first cell of the baby

 at one month, the baby is no bigger than a pea

 at three months, the baby is about 6 cm long

 at four months, the baby can move about

at five months, it sucks its thumb

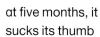
 at six months, the baby can hear sounds

at seven months, it opens its eyes and kicks strongly

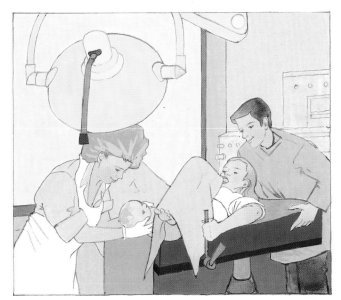

◁ When the baby is ready to be born, the mother may go to hospital to give birth. Her muscles help to push the baby out. Usually the baby comes out head first.

△ The doctor or midwife helps the baby to come out. The baby takes its first breath and cries. It does not need the umbilical cord after it is born, as it can get food and air from outside. So the cord is cut off.

at nine months, it is ready to be born

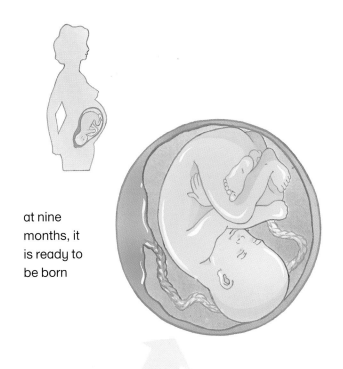

at eight months, it can taste things

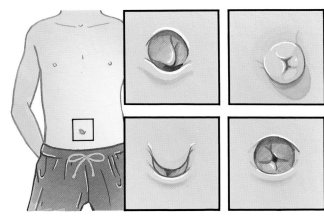

△ When the umbilical cord is cut, it leaves a scar. This becomes our navel, or bellybutton. Bellybuttons can be several different shapes, depending on how the cord was cut.

Growing up

It takes a long time for a baby to grow up. As it grows, it changes. Human beings keep changing all their lives. A new baby cannot look after itself, but it learns quickly. It becomes a child, then a teenager, then an adult. Adults may work and have children of their own. Then they become older. Their bodies start to get tired, and they do less.

Peter Pan
(A story by J.M. Barrie)

Peter Pan was not like other boys, he could fly and never grew any older.

◁ New babies need a lot of care and love. At first, they sleep a lot and cry when they are hungry.

▽ As babies grow, they do more and more things by themselves. First they crawl, then they walk.

△ Babies grow into children. They learn quickly, especially through play.

△ Children go to school. They do lessons, play games and make friends with other children.

▷ Children become teenagers. They are no longer children, but not yet adults.

▷ Teenagers grow into adult men and women. They can start work. There are lots of different jobs for them to do. They can also start a family.

▷ When they grow older, people retire, or stop work. Now they have time to relax and do things that they enjoy.

25

Seeing

The senses are ways that help us to know what is happening around us. Seeing is a sense. We see with our eyes.

Light comes into our eyes. It sends messages to the brain that then tells us what we see.

Our eyes are protected by eyelids and cleaned by tears.

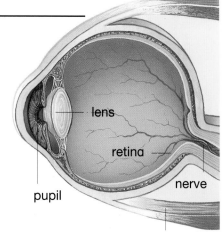

△ The pupil is the black circle in the centre of our eyes. It takes in light. Behind it are the lens, retina and nerves.

▷ The eye has muscles attached to it, so it can move up and down and side to side.

◁ Every time we blink, our eyelids spread tears over our eyes to keep them clean.

◁ In bright light, we need dark glasses to protect our eyes against the glare.

The Emperor's New Clothes
(A story by Hans Andersen)

The Emperor was tricked into wearing no clothes. He was told his new clothes were made out of special cloth that fools could not see. Really, no one could see the clothes.

pupil

△ When it is dark, our pupils grow larger. They do this to let in more light. This is to help us see better.

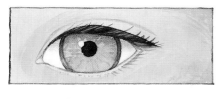

△ In daylight, the light is bright. Our pupils do not need to let in so much light, so they become smaller.

▷ Not everyone can see well. Sometimes we need help to make our sight better. That is why a lot of people wear glasses or contact lenses. These improve the eyesight.

glasses

contact lenses

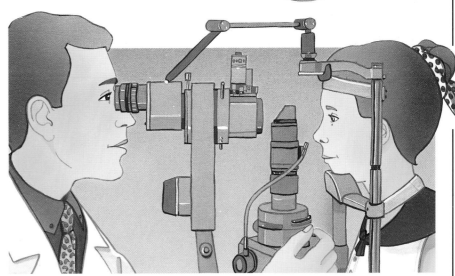

▽ Some people cannot see at all. They are blind. Some blind people have guide dogs to help them find their way.

△ Opticians look after people's eyes. They have special instruments to find out if anything is wrong. They can see through the pupil to the retina at the back of the eye.

Word box
Senses are the way we see, hear, smell, taste and touch the world around us.
Nerves carry messages to and fro between the brain and the different parts of the body.

27

Smelling

We use our noses to breathe and to smell. Smells float in the air. We smell things when we take in air through our noses. Smells are invisible, but our noses send messages to the brain, which tells us what they are.

Smells come from many different things around us. Some smells are nice, some are not. Our sense of smell also helps our sense of taste.

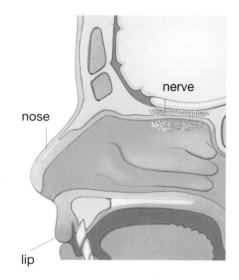

nerve

nose

lip

△ When a smell reaches the back of our nose, nerves tell the brain about it.

◁ There are some special doctors who look after people's noses, ears and throats only.

◁ If our nose is blocked and we cannot smell things, it is hard to taste them.

Can you find?

1 cheese
2 flower
3 soap
4 car exhaust
   fumes
5 scent

Find the answers

What do we use the nose for?

Why can you not see smells?

Tasting

We taste things with our tongues. There are thousands of little bumps all over the tongue called taste buds. Inside them are nerves that send messages to the brain about what we are eating. There are four main types of taste: sweet, salty, bitter and sour. Each is tasted by different parts of the tongue and mouth. The tongue is also able to feel heat, cold and pain.

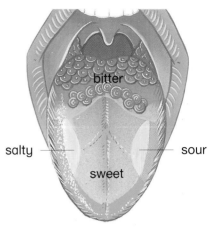

△ Different parts of the tongue are good at picking up different tastes. There are taste buds at the front, back and sides of the tongue.

△ The front of the tongue tastes sweet things mainly.

△ The sides taste salty things.

△ The sides also taste sour things.

△ The back tastes bitter things mainly.

Try tasting without smelling
Put water in four cups. Add salt to one, lemon juice to another and sugar to another. Leave the fourth. Ask a friend to hold their nose and taste them. See if they can tell the difference. Without smell, they should all taste the same.

Hearing

We hear sounds all the time. They tell us about the world around us. Sounds are vibrations in the air. We cannot see them. We hear sounds through our ears.

We can only see a part of the ear, the part that is outside the head. The rest of the ear is inside the head.

Some people cannot hear very well. People who cannot hear well are deaf.

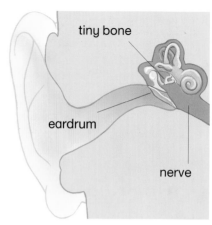

tiny bone

eardrum

nerve

△ Sounds make the eardrum move. This makes three tiny bones move. A nerve carries the message to the brain.

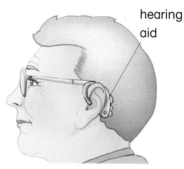

hearing aid

▽ There are all sorts of different sounds around us. Builders need to wear earmuffs to protect their ears from very loud sounds.

◁ A hearing aid helps people who cannot hear very well. It is a small machine which goes into the ear and makes sounds louder.

Helen Keller

Helen Keller could not hear, speak or see. She learnt to listen to people by placing her fingers on their lips and throat and feeling the vibrations that their voice made.

Touching

When we touch things, we can feel them. We can feel heat, cold, pain, softness, hardness and sharpness. Nerves just under the surface of the skin help us to feel things. They send messages to the brain about what we touch. We can feel best with the tips of our fingers because that is the place where we have the most nerves.

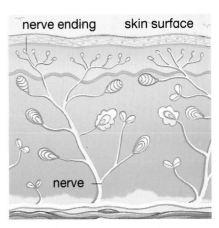

△ Tiny nerves in the skin send the brain messages about the things we touch. Nerves end just under the skin surface.

△ When we hold a drink of hot cocoa we can feel the heat through the cup.

▽ This blind person can read and write Braille, by using her sense of touch.

△ Pianists use their sense of touch to control sound. They can play softly or loudly depending on the pressure.

△ If we touch a thorn we feel a sharp prick on our fingers.

Feely game
Put some objects in a bag. They should all feel different. Ask your friends to put their hands in the bag and feel them. They must guess what the objects are by touch alone.

Breathing

We need air that contains oxygen to stay alive. The lungs take oxygen from the air we inhale, or breathe in. They also exhale, or breathe out, used air. Blood takes the oxygen from the lungs and carries it to the rest of the body.

The lungs work very hard. Every day we take about 23,000 breaths!

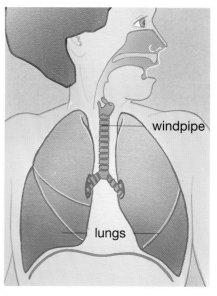

△ When you inhale, or breathe in, air goes down the windpipe into the lungs. Blood in the lungs collects oxygen and takes it around the body.

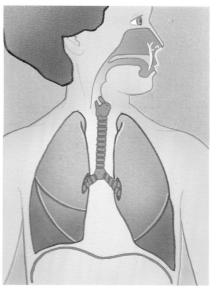

△ Blood also carries used air back to the lungs. When you exhale, or breathe out, your lungs push used air back out through your nose or mouth.

Word box
Inhale is what we do when we breathe in. The lungs become bigger and the air rushes in.
Exhale is what we do when we breathe out. The lungs become smaller, pushing the air out again.

△ Exercising in fresh mountain air is good for us. The air is cleaner than in the cities where there are often fumes from traffic and factories.

The Three Little Pigs
(An English folk tale)

Three little pigs each built a home. The first built a house of straw. The second built one of twigs. The third used bricks. A wicked wolf blew down the first two houses. But his lungs and breath were not strong enough to blow down the brick house.

◁ It is impossible to stay underwater without a snorkel or air tank, because there is no air to breathe. Most of us need to breathe at least 20 times a minute.

Blow football game
Make two goal posts with straws, using plasticine as shown. Place one at each end of a table. Make a scrunched-up paper ball. Each player chooses a home goal. The idea is to blow the ball into the other player's goal. Each goal scored earns one point. Play for five minutes. The winner is the one with the most points.

△ People who have asthma may use an inhaler to help them to breathe. Their air passages are narrower than usual. This causes noisy breathing or wheezing. The inhaler puffs or squirts a drug which makes their air passages wider, so they can breathe more easily.

Talking

We can talk, shout, laugh and sing. The sounds come out of our mouths. They are made by vocal cords in our throats. We move our tongue, lips and jaws to form words.

Sometimes we do not need words to show how we feel. We use our bodies instead. Our faces, hands and the way we move, all give messages to other people.

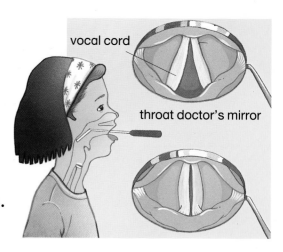

vocal cord

throat doctor's mirror

△ Our vocal cords are two stretchy flaps. The air that we breathe out moves them. This makes sounds.

▷ The way people stand and move, the movements of their hands, and the looks on their faces all show how they feel. This is called body language.

Can you find?

1 happy
2 sad
3 playful
4 silly
5 teasing
6 angry
7 tired
8 proud
9 worried

△ Singing is one way that we use our voices. Their sounds make music. Most people can sing, but some are better than others.

▷ The harder we breathe out, the louder our voice is. We can feel our throat move when we are singing.

◁ Some people cannot speak. They use their hands to make sign language instead.

Guess how they feel

You can often tell how people feel by the expressions, or looks, on their faces. Look at the faces below. Try and decide what these people are feeling by the way they look. Ask your friends what they think.

Blood supply

Blood flows around the body through thin tubes called veins and arteries. It carries oxygen from the air we breathe in and goodness from food that we eat. It also helps to fight germs. The heart is a hollow muscle that pumps blood each time it beats. It must be strong enough to send blood to every cell in the body.

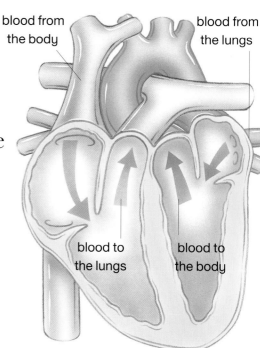

blood from the body

blood from the lungs

blood to the lungs

blood to the body

△ One side of the heart receives blood from the body and sends it to the lungs to collect oxygen. The other side receives blood carrying oxygen back from the lungs. This is then pumped around the body.

heart

artery

vein

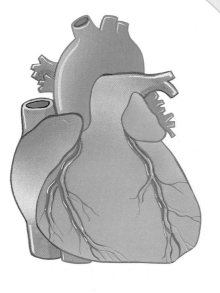

◁ The heart beats about 70 times each minute.

Make a stethoscope

A doctor uses a stethoscope to listen to patients' heartbeats. To make your own stethoscope, push a piece of tubing over the end of a funnel, as shown. Hold the funnel to your patient's chest and put the tubing near your ear. You will be able to hear their heartbeat.

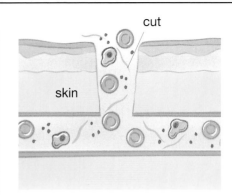

△ When you cut yourself, the white cells attack any germs that get in and platelets rush to plug the cut blood vessels.

white cell   platelet

▷ Blood contains red cells, white cells and platelets in a liquid called plasma. Red cells carry oxygen and white cells help fight germs. Platelets help the blood to clot.

plasma

red cell

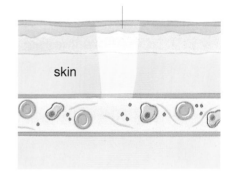

blood clot   scab

skin

△ A sticky clot is formed. This hardens into a scab that protects the wound.

healed cut

skin

△ As the wound heals, new skin grows underneath. This is pink when the scab drops off.

Find the answers

What does a scab do?

How many times does the heart beat a minute?

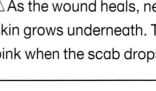
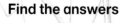

The nervous system

Nerves all through our bodies take messages from our senses to the brain. This is called the nervous system. The brain is the most important part of the body because it tells it how to work. It helps us to feel things and to think, learn and remember. Part of the brain also helps us to balance.

▽ Your brain helps you to think and concentrate.

▽ Your brain helps you to move at different speeds.

▽ It helps you to learn how to swim.

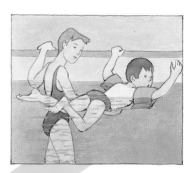

▽ It helps you to keep your balance.

▽ It helps you to walk and to talk.

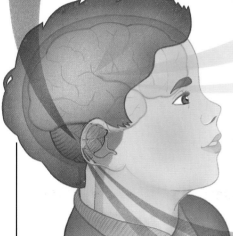

Play the memory game

Ask a friend to put ten objects on a tray. There could be a watch, a cup, a pen, a coin, a book and so on. Look at the tray for one minute, then cover it up. Write down all the things you saw. Can you remember every single one?

brain

spinal cord

nerve

▷Messages from our senses pass through the nerves to the spinal cord. This is a thick bundle of nerves down the middle of our backs. It carries signals to the brain. Then the brain sends messages along other nerves that tell the body what to do.

△Sometimes the nervous system reacts very quickly. This happens when you are in danger of hurting yourself.

△When you touch something sharp, your hand will jerk away. You do not have to think about it. This is called a reflex action.

◁When you learn something, the brain stores it so that you can remember it another time. This is called memory.

Eating for energy

We eat food because it gives our bodies energy. People eat many different kinds of food, but our bodies use everything in the same way. When you swallow food, it moves down a tube into the stomach and then into the intestines. On the way, the goodness is taken out of the food. This is called digestion.

The Magic Porridge Pot
(A story by the Brothers Grimm)

A lady gave a tired, hungry girl a magic pot and told her magic words to make the pot cook delicious, nourishing porridge. But when the girl's mother used the magic pot she forgot how to stop it. The porridge flooded the whole village! When the girl stopped the pot, they had to eat their way into their home!

gullet

stomach

small intestine

large intestine

◁ Food goes down the gullet to the stomach, which mashes it·up. Then it is squeezed along the intestines. It passes through the intestine walls into the blood. Solid fibre passes through as waste when all the goodness has been taken out.

△ In different parts of the world, people eat different types of food. All of it gives the body the energy it needs to live.

Getting rid of waste

As your body works, it makes waste products. The body has to get rid of them. It does this in several ways. We exhale, or breathe out, used air from our lungs. When we sweat we get rid of salt and other waste. We go to the toilet to get rid of urine from our bladders and solid waste from our bowels.

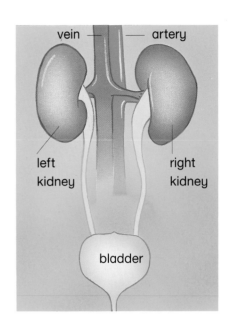

Our waste

We have to go to the toilet to get rid of urine and solid waste. When our bowels are full we get rid of solid waste. When our bladder is full we get rid of urine. The bladder can store up to three quarters of a pint of liquid. If we drink a lot our bladders fill up because the body does not need most of the water. If we drink less, or lose a lot of water from sweating, the kidneys make less urine.

△ Blood flows through the kidneys. The kidneys take water, salt and other waste from the blood. This waste is turned into urine and stored in a pouch called the bladder.

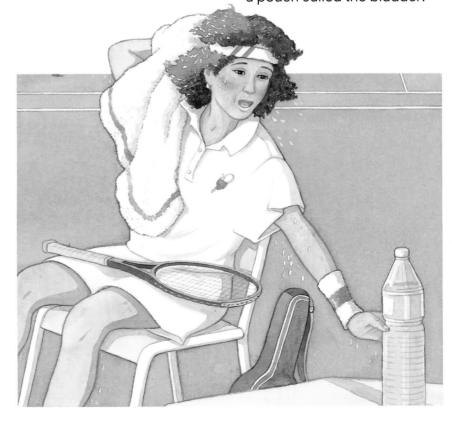

▷ Sweat is a liquid that comes out of our skin. It gets rid of waste and cools us down.

Healthy eating

Your food should give your body what it needs to keep working. This is called nutrition. There are four main groups of food, called proteins, carbohydrates, fats and fibre. Your body needs food from each group and water to drink. It also needs the vitamins in food.

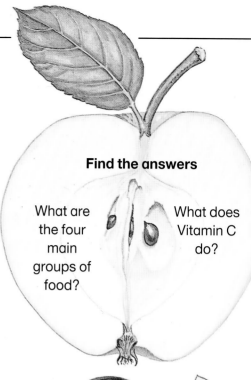

Find the answers

What are the four main groups of food?

What does Vitamin C do?

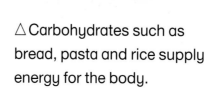

△ Proteins such as meat, eggs and beans help the body to stay strong.

△ Carbohydrates such as bread, pasta and rice supply energy for the body.

△ Fats such as butter, milk, cheese and oils store energy for the body to use later.

△ Vitamin B comes from these foods. It gives energy and healthy skin.

△ Vitamin A comes from these foods. It gives us good eyesight and healthy skin.

△ These fruit and vegetables give us a lot of fibre. They also give us Vitamin C which helps us recover from illness and injury.

△ Vitamin E comes from these foods. It helps the body's cells stay strong.

△ Vitamin D comes from these foods. It helps us to grow properly.

	breakfast	lunch	tea
Mon	cereal	cheese sandwiches	beans on toast apple
Tues	egg	peanut butter sandwich	pizza apple
Wed	toast		
Thurs			
Fri			
Sat			
Sun			

△ Vitamin K comes from these foods. It stops us bleeding too much if we get a cut.

Keep a food diary

Every day for a week, write down what you eat for breakfast, lunch and tea. Then look at the pictures on this page. Are you eating something from every food group each day? What sort of foods do you eat most?

Word box
Nutrition is the process of eating and using the food for growth, energy and keeping our body working.
Vitamins are found in food. Our body needs them to stay healthy.

Teeth

We bite into food and chew it with our teeth so it is easier to swallow. Our teeth are different shapes and they do different things. Teeth are fixed into our jaws, but they can come loose. Children lose their first teeth and grow another, larger set. If we do not brush our teeth, they will rot, or decay.

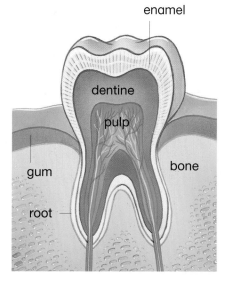

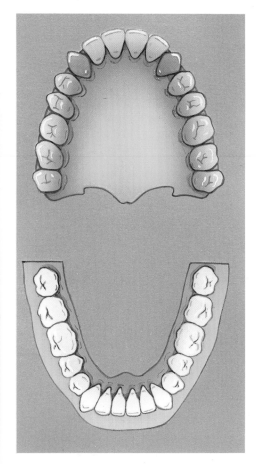

△ The sharp incisors at the front are for cutting food. Pointed canines at the sides tear it. Big molars at the back crush it.

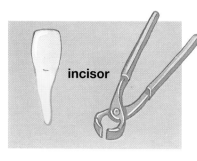

△ Incisors cut like pliers.

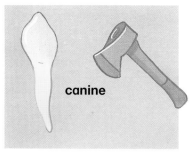

△ Canines cut like an axe.

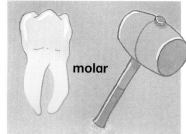

△ Molars crush like a hammer.

△ The outside of the tooth is a hard layer of enamel. This covers the dentine. Inside this is the pulp. Roots hold the tooth in place in the jawbone.

The Tooth Fairy
Some people say that if you lose a tooth, you should put it under your pillow. Then the Tooth Fairy will come and take it away. Sometimes the Tooth Fairy leaves money in exchange for the tooth.

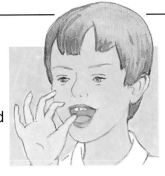  

▷When we are about six years old, our first teeth become loose and fall out. Larger teeth grow underneath.

◁The dentist looks after our teeth. If he finds a decaying tooth, he removes the decay and fills the hole with hard paste.

Make an eggshell decay

Ask an adult to hard boil an egg. Put it in a cup of malt vinegar. Leave it for a day, then see how much of the shell has been eaten away by the vinegar. This is what fizzy drinks and sweets do to your teeth.

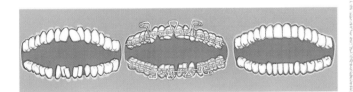

△Some people wear a brace or a plate to make crooked teeth straight.

 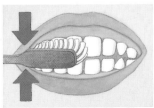 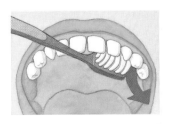 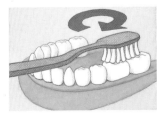

△Brush your teeth for three minutes.

△Brush up and down the front of your teeth.

△Then brush up and down the back.

△Always brush with a circular movement.

Healthy life

If we want to be healthy, we should always look after our body. It needs to be kept clean. The skin gets dirty, so we should wash every day and change our clothes too.

Plenty of exercise is good for most people. Sports and games help our bodies to grow stronger and fitter.

△ To keep clean, it helps to change our clothes when they are dirty, and put on clean ones.

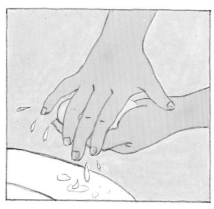

△ Washing in soap and water helps get rid of germs.

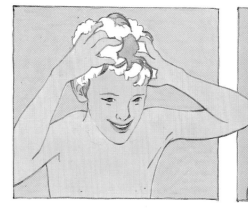

△ Washing our hair keeps it clean and shiny.

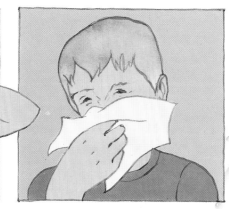

△ Blowing our noses gets rid of dirt and keeps it clean.

△ Clean your ears gently. Never use sharp objects.

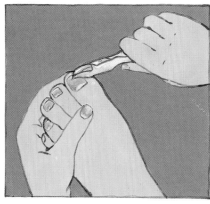

△ Toenails must be cut, or they will grow too long.

Find the answers

Name two mountain sports and two water sports.

Why do we wash?

46

▷In very high mountains there is nearly always snow. This means that in these places people can enjoy sledging and skiing for most of the year.

◁Running is a very popular sport. It makes all the muscles in our bodies stronger. If we do it regularly, we will be fitter and will not get tired or out of breath.

▷Water sports are activities that we do in the sea or in the swimming pool. Swimming and diving are water sports. We can also float in the water or do exercises.

◁Whichever sport we choose, we have to follow the rules and concentrate to do well. When we play in a team, we should think of others, so that everybody has fun.

Sleep

We all need to sleep. Sleep allows the body to rest and gain strength after a busy day. Most children sleep for about twelve hours every night. Babies need even more sleep, because they are growing very quickly and this makes their bodies tired. Adults need less sleep as they are no longer growing. If we do not have enough sleep, we may become grumpy.

Find the answers

How many hours sleep do most children need?

What are frightening dreams called?

Why do we change position while we sleep?

△ While you are asleep, your body keeps working slowly. Slowing down helps it to rest a little and grow strong.

▷ You do not lie completely still all night, but change position many times. If you were to lie in one place, you would ache in the morning.

Sleeping Beauty
(A story by Charles Perrault)

A wicked witch cast a spell on Sleeping Beauty just after she was born. Years later, having pricked her finger, she and everyone in her castle, fell asleep. One hundred years passed before a prince kissed her and broke the spell. They fell in love and got married.

△ While we are asleep, we have dreams. The stories in our dreams seem real while we are asleep. But we do not always remember them when we wake up. Often we dream about things we have seen or done the day before.

△ Nightmares are frightening dreams. Some nightmares are so frightening that they wake us up. But often nightmares can be useful, because they help sort out some of the fears and worries we have in real life.

When you are ill

When you are ill, you may have a high temperature, a cough, spots, or aches and pains. These are signs that your body is being attacked by germs. Germs are tiny living things that float in air and water. They can make you ill if they get inside your body.

Doctors can give you vaccinations that fight germs and prevent illness.

Find the answers

Why do you get hot if you are ill?

What does the doctor use to listen to your lungs?

▽ When your body is fighting off invading germs, it works harder. Your heart beats faster. It pumps more blood around your body. This makes you get hot and you may sweat. It is called having a temperature.

stethoscope

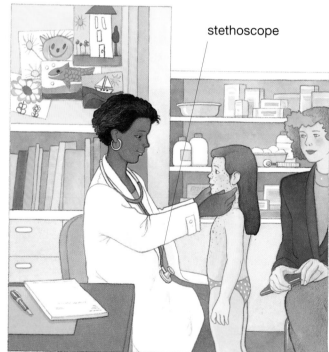

thermometer

△ The doctor examines you. She listens to your heart and lungs with a stethoscope, looks in your ears and throat, and asks you questions. The doctor may give you medicine to help fight the germs. Remember that you should only take medicines given to you by your doctor.

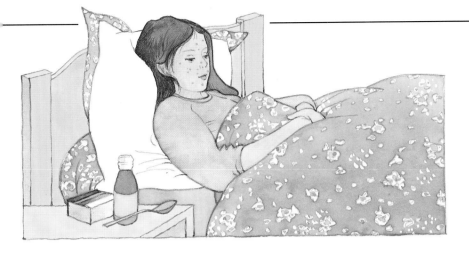

◁ Some diseases, such as chickenpox, are very easy to catch, but you usually catch them only once. After that, the body learns to protect itself against the disease.

▷ If you have already had chickenpox, you are safe to visit a friend who is ill with it. Your body recognizes the disease and can fight it, so you do not catch it again.

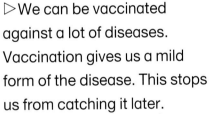

Play spotty faces
Draw two large faces on card. Put 20 counters on each face. These are the spots. Take turns to throw a dice. If you throw a six, take six spots from your face, and so on. The first with no spots left wins.

▷ We can be vaccinated against a lot of diseases. Vaccination gives us a mild form of the disease. This stops us from catching it later.

A happy life

Love and friendship and respect for each other make life happy for everyone. One way of showing these feelings is with our bodies. A cuddle, a kiss, a hug, a smile, a wave or an outstretched hand are all things we can do that bring happiness.

Index

This index will help you to find out where you can read information about a subject. It is in alphabetical order. Each section is under a large letter of the alphabet. A main entry and its page numbers are printed in **dark**, or **bold**, letters. This is where you will find the most information. Below a main entry, there may be a second list. This shows other places in the book where you can find further information on your subject.